FRONT VIEW OF MOUNT VERNON MANSION AS IT APPEARS TODAY

Mount Vernon and the Washington Family

A concise handbook on the ancestry, youth and family of George Washington, and history of his home

Fifth and Enlarged Edition		Illustrated and Indexed

Prepared for the busy reader who does not have time to peruse voluminous works on these subjects.

By

C. Hale Sipe, A.B.

of the Pittsburgh and Butler, Pennsylvania Bars; Member of
the Historical Society of Pennsylvania; Author of
"The Indian Chiefs of Pennsylvania" and
"The Indian Wars of Pennsylvania"

THE ZIEGLER PRINTING CO., INC.,
BUTLER, PA.
1929

973.410924
Si7m

Preface

(*Preface to Third Edition*)

THE PURPOSE of this book is to tell clearly, concisely, and accurately the leading facts in George Washington's ancestry, his youth, his household, and his Mount Vernon Estate; and it is confidently asserted that more information concerning these subjects is given herein than can be found elsewhere in a like space.

The very gratifying reception given former editions of this work during the past year, and the many requests for a more detailed treatment of the subjects appearing in the former editions, are the reasons for the work now appearing in a larger form.

Among the authorities consulted in the preparation of the volume are:

Washington Irving's "Life of Washington",
Schroeder-Lossing "Life of Washington",
Sparks' "Life of Washington",
Headley's "Life of Washington",
Headley's "Washington and His Generals",
Snowden's "Some Old Historic Landmarks of Virginia and Maryland",
Ford's "True George Washington",
Wilstach's "Mount Vernon",
Lossing's "Mount Vernon", and
Callahan's "Washington, The Man and Mason".

The volume is sent on its mission with the hope that its readers may be led to a more extensive study of the life of George Washington, of whom the great Gladstone said:

"HE IS THE PUREST FIGURE IN HISTORY."

C. HALE SIPE,
July, 1925.   Butler, Pennsylvania.

CONTENTS

———

LIST OF ILLUSTRATIONS

———

Mount Vernon and the Washington Family

Origin of the Name "Washington"

The Washington family is of English origin. In the year 1183, the noble Knight, William de Hertburn, a Chevalier in the train of the Count Palatinate, Bishop of Durham, received a grant of the manor of Wessyngton, in the County of Durham in the northern part of England. As was usual in those days, the de Hertburn family took the name of the estate and was called de Wessyngton. By degrees the seignioral sign "de" disappeared from before the family surname. In like manner the orthography of the surname passed through modifications of "Wessyngton", "Wassington", "Weschington", and "Wasshington", and eventually attained its familiar modern form of Washington. From this William de Hertburn, or de Wessyngton, have descended the various branches of the Washington family in England and America.

The history of the manor of Wessyngton goes back to the Danish Conquest, when some Vikings established a settlement called Wassa—inga—tun. The name means "the settlement of the sons of Wassa."

Although George Washington's pedigree was one of which any person could be proud, yet he manifested very little interest in the same. His attitude toward the subject of pedigree finds expression in the words of Daniel Webster: "No one but a shallow minded pretender would either make distinguished origin a matter of personal merit or obscure origin a matter of personal reproach."

After Washington was elevated to the presidency of

the United States, he received a letter on the subject of his ancestry from Sir Isaac Heard, then Garter King at Arms in London, who was anxious to inquire into the family line of the great American. Washington replied thanking Sir Isaac for the trouble he had taken in making the genealogical collections relative to the Washington Family, but stating: "This is a subject to which, I confess, I have paid very little attention. My time has been so much occupied in the busy and active scenes of life, from an early period of it, that but a small portion could have been devoted to researches of this nature, even if my inclination or particular circumstances should have prompted to the inquiry."

He was unable to trace his ancestry further than his great grandfather, the John Washington mentioned in another statement in his reply to the letter of Sir Isaac Heard: "In the year 1657, or thereabouts, and during the usurpation of Oliver Cromwell, John and Lawrence Washington, brothers, emigrated from the north of England, and settled at Bridges Creek on the Potomac in the County of Westmoreland. But from whom they descended, the subscriber is possessed of no document to ascertain."

Ancient Home of the Washingtons

Sulgrave Manor, in Northamptonshire, in the central part of England, was the home of some of George Washington's remote ancestors for a number of generations. In 1538 Lawrence Washington, of Gray's Inn, who was at one time Mayor of Northampton, received a grant of the Manor of Sulgrave after Henry the Eighth's dissolution of the priories. Sulgrave, on account of its being the home of the Washington family, was called "Washington's Manor." The Manor house is still standing and is visited by thousands of tourists.

Lawrence Washington, the first proprietor of Sulgrave Manor, was the great great-grandfather of the first of Washington's ancestors to come to America. His son, Robert Washington, of Sulgrave, was the father of Lawrence Washington, also of Sulgrave; and this Lawrence was the father of Reverend Lawrence Washington, Rector of Purleigh, in Essex in the southeastern part of England, whose son John Washington, emigrated to the Colony of Virginia.

To such persons as may desire to trace George Washington's paternal ancestry beyond Lawrence Washington, the first proprietor of Sulgrave Manor, it may be interesting to know that this Lawrence was the eldest son of John Washington, of Wharton, who was the son of John Washington, of Whitfield, in the County of Lancaster, whose father was John Washington, also of Whitfield.

Among Washington's English ancestors were many persons of note—men who won fame as scholars and soldiers. In addition to William de Hertburn, there were the following distinguished members of the Washington family in England: William Washington, a loyal and devoted defender of Henry the III. in the wars of the Barons; Sir Stephen de Wessington, one of the Chevaliers of Edward III; Sir William, of the Privy Council of Durham; John the learned prior of the Benedictines, author of "De Juribus et Possessionibus Ecclesiae Dunelm"; Lieutenant-Colonel James Washington, a loyal subject of Charles I. who died for his king at the siege of Pontefract; Joseph Washington, an eminent lawyer who translated one of Milton's political treatises and a part of "Lucian's Dialogues"; and Sir Henry Washington, famous for his daring at the storming of Bristol and the siege of Worcester.

As we shall find when we trace the history of Washington's American ancestors, the military qualities of the

English Washingtons were perpetuated by their American descendants, from the very first one who emigrated to the new world.

John Washington, the Immigrant

As stated above, the first of the Washingtons to come to America, was John, son of Rev. Lawrence Washington. The father was educated at Oxford, held the degree Master of Arts, and was rector of Purleigh to which parish a very good living was attached. He was a Royalist, and, in the political upheaval attendant upon the decline of the Stuart dynasty and the rise of the Puritan power, his fortunes waned. Finally the Puritan Parliament ejected him from his comfortable living, and he was obliged to serve as rector at Brixted Parva, a parish where the living was "such a poor and miserable one that it was with difficulty that any one was persuaded to accept it."

The rector with his good wife Amphillis Rhodes and their issue of six children now facing poverty, the eldest son John, the great-grandfather of the immortal George Washington, early left home, and later, with his wife and two children, emigrated from South Cave in the East Riding of Yorkshire, near the city of Beverly, in the northeastern part of England. Arriving in Virginia in 1658, he patented a large tract of land in Westmoreland County, a little over seventy miles down the Potomac from our present National Capital. His brother Lawrence and a sister also came to Virginia, but whether they accompanied him or arrived shortly after is not clearly established.

John Washington is known in history as "John Washington, the Immigrant". He first settled on a plantation between the Rappahannock and the Potomac giving the name of "Washington" to the parish in which he resided.

Soon after his arrival, his wife and two children died. In 1660, he married a second wife, Anne Pope, the daughter of a neighboring planter. Some authorities assert that she had been married before to Walter Brodhurst and was a widow at the time of her marriage to Washington.

After his second marriage, Mr. Washington took up his permanent residence at Bridges Creek, Westmoreland County, near where this stream flows into the Potomac, on a plantation later named "Wakefield". The estate stretched along the Potomac more than a mile between Pope's and Bridge's Creek, and consisted of more than one thousand acres.

"Wakefield" was destined to be the ancestral home of the American Washingtons and the birthplace of George Washington. Here John Washington, "the Immigrant", died in 1677, and here his dust reposes. Here were born all his children by his second marriage: Lawrence, the eldest, grandfather of George Washington, born in 1661; John, born in 1663; Elizabeth, born in 1665, and Anne, born in 1667. Here also reposes the dust of Lawrence. Here all Lawrence's children were born; John, born in 1692; Augustine, father of the Revolutionary General, born in 1694; and Mildred, born in 1696. Augustine's dust, too, reposes in Wakefield's hallowed soil.

Here George Washington first saw the light of day on February 22, 1732 (Old Style February 11). The family Bible contains the following record:

> "George Washington, son of Augustine and Mary, his wife, was born the 11th day of February, 1731-2, about 10 in the morning; and was baptized the 3″ of April following: Mr. Beverly Whiting and Captain Christopher Brooks, Godfathers; and Mrs. Mildred Gregory, Godmother."

Mildred Gregory, the Godmother at Washington's baptism, was his aunt, a sister of his father. She was the wife of Roger Gregory.

Not a vestige of the house in which George Washington was born now remains. It was a primitive farmhouse of Virginia, having a steep roof which sloped down into low projecting eaves. It contained four rooms on the first floor, and others in the attic, and had an immense chimney at each end. In it, as above stated, both his father and his grandfather were born. It was delightfully situated about seventy miles down the Potomac from the Capital, commanding a beautiful view of the majestic and historic river and the Maryland shores beyond.

A suitable monument, erected in 1895, now marks the spot where the house stood, but for many years the site was marked by a slab of freestone, lying horizontally, and placed there in June, 1815, by George Washington Parke Custis, bearing the following inscription:

"HERE, THE 11TH OF FEBRUARY, 1732,
GEORGE WASHINGTON WAS BORN."

A final word as to John Washington, "the Immigrant". He became a man of wealth and prominence in the colony, taking a leading part in the commercial, political and military affairs of Virginia. He was an extensive planter and proprietor of several large plantations. In 1670 he and Nicholas Spencer became associated in an enterprise with the mother country in bringing one hundred settlers into the virgin wilds of the colony. In consideration of the valuable services rendered to the colony in this project, he and Spencer received from Thomas, Lord Culpepper a grant of five thousand acres of land on the Potomac between Dogue Run, or Epsewasson, and Little

Hunting Creeks—a tract which was later divided between his heirs and the heirs of Spencer, as will be more fully shown when we relate the history of Mount Vernon, the part thereof allotted to the Washingtons since becoming known throughout the civilized world as "Mount Vernon on the Potomac", the home of George Washington and the shrine of America.

About 1665 he was elected to the House of Burgesses and was commissioned a Colonel in the colonial militia. His most important military service consisted in leading an expedition of fifteen hundred Virginia and Maryland militia against a force of twenty-five hundred Indians of Virginia and Maryland who had committed outrages in Virginia and, when pursued, entrenched themselves with an allied tribe, on a high bluff overlooking the Potomac on the present site of Fort Washington. Colonel Washington dislodged the savages and drove them over "the great wall" into the valley of the Shennandoah.

Upon his death he willed the homestead at Wakefield and his share in the Epsewasson, or Mount Vernon tract, to his eldest son Lawrence, whose fortunes we shall now trace. We shall make no effort to follow the diverging lines of descent through each of the children of John Washington "the Immigrant" but shall follow the direct line from him to the "Father of his Country", digressing now and then as side lights of our narrative may require.

Lawrence Washington, Grandfather of the General

Lawrence lived on the ancestral plantation all his life. He married Mildred, daughter of Colonel Augustine Warner, of Gloucester County, and died at Wakefield in March, 1698, at the early age of thirty-seven years. His children, as stated on page 15, were all born on the ancestral plantation; but only one of them, Augustine, father of the Revolutionary General, found a grave in its soil.

Lawrence Washington was a man of wealth. By his will probated March 30th, 1698, he divided the rest of his personal property after making a number of bequests to friends and relatives, equally among his wife and three children. He willed his real estate as follows: To his eldest son John he gave the ancestral home at Wakefield; to Mildred he gave his share in the twenty-five hundred acre tract on Hunting Creek, later known as Mount Vernon, and to Augustine he gave the rest of his landed estate.

After the death of Lawrence, his widow moved to England, where she married George Gale, of Whitehaven, Cumberland County, at which place she died in January, 1701. In her will probated March 18th, 1701, she divided the rest of her estate equally among her husband and three children after first giving the husband a specific bequest of one thousand pounds. The husband, who became her executor and the guardian of his three step-children, placed the two boys, John and Augustine Washington, in the school at Appleby, near his home.

In 1712 Mr. Gale emigrated to Maryland, bringing the step-children with him. A few years later John married Katherine Whiting, of Gloucester County, Virginia, where he settled on a plantation called "Highgate" on the Pianketank River. He became a colonel in the Virginia militia. He, like his ancestors, was a churchman, being a vestryman in Petsworth parish. He died on September 1st, 1746. His son, Warner, married Hannah, daughter of William Fairfax, of Belvoir, near Mount Vernon.

Mildred married first Roger Gregory, of Stafford

County, Virginia, and second, Colonel Henry Willis, who founded the City of Fredericksburg. As the wife of Roger Gregory, she was the Godmother at the Baptism of her nephew, George Washington. We shall now trace the history of Augustine.

Augustine, the Father of Washington

Augustine Washington, as stated above, was the second child of Lawrence Washington and his wife, Mildred Warner. He resided on the ancestral plantation at Wakefield until 1735, having purchased this farm from his brother John of "Highgate" in Gloucester County. Then he moved to the Hunting Creek, or Mount Vernon estate, purchased from his sister Mildred, where he resided until 1739, in which year he took up his abode on his "Pine Grove" plantation on the Rappahannock.

Augustine Washington was twice married. His first wife was Jane, daughter of Caleb Butler, of Westmoreland County, whom he married on April 20, 1715, and who died at Wakefield on November 24, 1728. His second wife whom he married March 6, 1730, and who became the mother of George Washington, was Mary, the youngest daughter of Col. Joseph Ball, of Lancaster County, whose plantation was near the mouth of the Rappahannock.

By his first marriage, Augustine was the father of the following children: Butler, born in 1716; Lawrence, born in 1718; Augustine, born in 1720, and Jane, born in 1722. All these children were born at Wakefield.

Augustine's children by his second marriage were: George, born February 22nd, 1732; Elizabeth (Betty), born June 20, 1733; Samuel, born November 16, 1734; John Augustine, born January 13, 1736; Charles, born May 2, 1738, and Mildred, born June 21, 1739.

George, Elizabeth, and Samuel were born at Wakefield; John Augustine, Charles and Mildred were born at Mount Vernon.

Augustine was a Virginia planter of the better class. He was a man of liberal attainments, having been educated at Appleby School in England. He took an active part in the affairs of the Colony, and was a member of the House of Burgesses. His landed possessions were large,

OLD BARN AT MOUNT VERNON
Very likely built by Washington's father, Augustine Washington.

including the ancestral home at Wakefield, an estate on the east side of the Rappahannock, nearly opposite Fredericksburg, and the estate on the Potomac later called Mount Vernon.

He was, in truth, a good man and deeply interested in the children's moral and religious education, being devoutly attached to the English Church. He was also a man of strong mind, with great energy of purpose.

In appearance, he was noble, with uncommon height,

and great muscular power. His thoughts and feelings were under the control of practical religion. On his death-bed he made the following utterance which honors his memory:

> "I thank God that, in all my life, I never struck a man in anger; for, if I had, I am sure that from my remarkable muscular powers I should have killed my antagonist, and then his blood, at this awful moment, would have lain heavily upon my soul. As it is, I die at peace with all mankind."

He died April 12, 1743, aged forty-nine years, on his "Pine Grove" plantation on the Rappahannock, to which the family had moved in 1739, as stated elsewhere; and his body was taken back to Wakefield, and placed in the ancestral vault. His immortal son, who was visiting his cousins, Robert and Lawrence Washington, at Chotank, during the father's fatal illness, reached home too late to hear his father utter a blessing, or a farewell, and just in time to receive a last feeble glance of recognition.

Augustine's children living at the time of his death were:

Lawrence and Augustine by his first wife, Jane Butler; and George, Elizabeth (Betty), John Augustine, Charles and Samuel, by his second wife, Mary Ball. He willed his estate as follows:

To Lawrence he gave the Hunting Creek, or Mount Vernon estate, and a tract of land on Maddox Creek in Westmoreland County. To Betty he gave two Negro children, with the provision that Lawrence was to pay her four hundred pounds in cash. To Augustine he gave the old homestead at Wakefield. To George he gave his Pine Grove plantation on the Rappahannock. To Samuel he gave six hundred acres of land on Chotank in Stafford County, together with an interest in land lying on Deep Run. To John Augustine he gave seven hundred acres of land on Maddox Creek, above named, and to Charles he gave seven hundred acres in Prince William County. The rest of his estate he divided between his wife, Mary Ball, and her children. He also gave her the crops then growing on his plantations at Wakefield, Pine Grove, and Chotank.

In a codicil to his will he gave George "one lot of land in the town of Fredericksburg."

Mary, the Mother of Washington

As said elsewhere, the mother of Washington was Mary, youngest daughter of Colonel Joseph Ball, of Lancaster County, Virginia. She was born on the banks of the Rappahannock in 1707 or 1708, and grew into lovely womanhood amid the sylvan scenes of her birthplace. When she married Augustine Washington in 1730, she was so celebrated for her beauty that she was known as the "Rose of Epping Forest."

She was the mother of six children, whose names are given elsewhere, and five of whom survived their father. The widowed mother was eminently qualified, by nature and religion, to fulfill all her duties to her family. She constantly sought to form the hearts and minds of her children according to the teachings of the New Testament, and tradition tells that she frequently read to them select parts of Sir Matthew Hale's "Contemplations, Moral and Divine," a work abounding in maxims of wisdom and piety. Therefore it was the lot of George

Washington to receive from his mother the advantages of a sound religious education.

After the death of her husband, she continued to reside on and manage the Rappahannock plantation until 1775,

Monument marking the grave of Washington's mother at Fredericksburg, Virginia. She died at Fredericksburg, August 25, 1789.

when her son George bought her a house in Fredericksburg, near "Kenmore", the residence of her daughter "Betty", the wife of Colonel Fielding Lewis. Here she spent the remainder of her days.

After her more than illustrious son had reached the highest pinnacle of fame in having led the Patriot Armies to victory, through the fire and blood of the Revolutionary War, she said to Lafayette, "I am not surprised at what George has done; he was always a good boy."

In December, 1783, Washington visited his mother in Fredericksburg. He had just resigned his commission as Commander-in-Chief of the American armies, and, as a private citizen, had come to pay a visit to his mother and the friends of his childhood. Military and civic

23

organizations turned out to do him honor. There were parades and the booming of cannon. The ceremonies were closed by a grand ball, which has gone down into history as the "peace ball". The mother of Washington attended, accompanied by her son, now the foremost man on the American continent. On the occasion of this visit he made an address in which he spoke of the honored matron as "my revered mother, by whose maternal hand, early deprived of a father, I was led to manhood."

She passed away August 25, 1789, and is buried within sight of her home in Fredericksburg, at a beautiful spot where she spent many hours in reading, meditation and prayer, in the latter years of her life. Above her grave is a granite monument, fifty feet high, bearing the simple inscription:

"MARY, THE MOTHER OF WASHINGTON"

George Washington was not present at the time of her death, being at the seat of government in New York City. Shortly before his departure from Mount Vernon in April, 1789, to take up his duties as the first president of the United States, he paid a visit to his mother, when he then saw her for the last time. Upon hearing of her death, he wrote thus to his sister, Betty:

"Awful and affecting as the death of a parent is, there is consolation in knowing that Heaven has spared ours to an age beyond which few attain, and favored her with full enjoyment of her faculties, and as much bodily strength as usually falls to the lot of four score. Under these circumstances, and in the hope that she is translated to a happier place, it is the duty of her relatives to yield submission to the decree of the Creator. When I was last at Fredericksburg, I took a final leave of my mother, never expecting to see her more."

The Brothers and Sisters of Washington

As shown elsewhere, George Washington had three brothers of the half-blood and one sister of the half-blood; also three brothers of the full-blood and two sisters of the full-blood. The dates of their birth have already been told. All of them preceded him in death. On learning of the death of his brother, Charles, in the autumn of 1799, whom he survived but a short time, he said: "I was the first and am now the last of my father's children, of the second marriage, who remain. When I shall be called upon to follow them is known only to the Giver of Life. When the summons comes I shall endeavor to obey it with good grace."

His half-brother, Butler, died in childhood, at Wakefield, and his half-sister, Jane, died at Mount Vernon on January 17, 1735, in her thirteenth year. His full-sister, Mildred, died October 23, 1740, on the father's "Pine Grove" plantation on the Rappahannock, aged a little more than one year. All the other brothers and sisters of both the half-blood and full-blood reached maturity.

Washington's half brother, Major Lawrence Washington, was a man of much prominence in the Colony of Virginia. He was one of the organizers of the "Ohio Company" formed for the purpose of exploring and settling the western country along the Ohio River. Fifteen years older than George, he took the place of a father to the fatherless boy. He inherited Mount Vernon, upon the death of the father, which he named in honor of

BETTY WASHINGTON, SISTER OF THE GENERAL
She married Colonel Fielding Lewis, of Fredericksburg. She was strikingly like
her brother in face and form. Died March 31, 1797.

Admiral Vernon, under whom he had fought at Cartagena, in South America, and it was his home from 1743 until his death. He married Anne, eldest daughter of Hon. William Fairfax, July 19, 1743. George took up his permanent residence with him here in the autumn of 1747. Never strong physically, his health gave way while yet in young manhood, and in 1751, accompanied by George, he went to the Island of Barbadoes in search of health. During their stay on the island, George contracted smallpox, which left his face pitted for life. Lawrence's search for health was in vain, and he hurried home by way of Bermuda in the summer of 1752 "in time to die under his own roof, (July 26, 1752), surrounded by his family and friends." He was laid to rest in the family burying ground at Mount Vernon by the side of his three infant children, and their bodies were later placed in the old vault.

To his half-brother, Augustine, in the only letter that now remains, Washington wrote: "The pleasure of your company at Mount Vernon always did and always will afford me infinite satisfaction." This letter is signed "Your most affectionate brother." Augustine married Ann Aylett in 1743, and died in 1760 at Wakefield, where he is buried.

His sister Betty was strikingly like him in face and figure. She married Colonel Fielding Lewis, as stated elsewhere. Between her and Washington there existed a strong attachment. During the Revolutionary War, she wrote him thus: "Oh, when will that day arrive when we shall meet again. Trust the Lord it will be soon,—till then you have the prayers and kind wishes for your health and happiness of your loving and sincerely affectionate sister." Her husband was a man of large fortune and great prominence in the Colony. During the Revolu-

27

tion, the Virginia Assembly appointed him Chief Commissioner for the Manufacture of Small Arms. Washington was a frequent visitor at "Kenmore", the home of the Lewises, at Fredericksburg. Betty Lewis died, March 31, 1797, while visiting her daughter at Western View, Culpepper County, Virginia, and is buried at that place.

Samuel, the eldest of his brothers of the full blood, seems to have had extravagant tendencies, which got him into pecuniary difficulties. He made many requests for loans from his brother which seem to have been always granted. It is clear that these requests were annoying to George. In 1781, he wrote to another brother, "In God's name how did my brother Samuel get himself so enormously in debt?" These loans were not paid back at the time of George Washington's death, and, in his will, he discharged the estate of Samuel from obligation to pay them.

Samuel first temporarily resided in Westmoreland County, but about the year 1768, he moved to the Valley of Virginia, taking up his abode in Berkeley (now Jefferson) County, West Virginia, where he died on his plantation called "Harewood" in 1781, where he is buried. He was a vestryman in Norborne Parish and a member of the Justice Court in 1771. He also served in the Revolutionary War, as Colonel. Samuel was married five times. His first wife was Jane Champe; the second, Mildred Thornton; the third, Lucy Chapman; the fourth, Anne Allerton, and the fifth, Susanna Perrin.

Washington's brother Charles at first resided in Westmoreland County, and in 1768 moved, like Samuel, to Berkely (now Jefferson) County, West Virginia, where he built a mansion called "Mordington." He took a prominent part in the affairs of his adopted county. In 1786, he and several associates founded the City of Charlestown,

West Virginia, which was located on his land and named for him. Charles married Mildred Thornton. He died at "Mordington" in 1799, just a few months prior to the death of his illustrious brother. His dust reposes at "Mordington".

His full-brother John Augustine, Washington describes in his will as "the intimate companion of my youth, and the friend of my ripened age." With this brother he always corresponded, addressing him affectionately as "Dear Jack" and signing himself "Your loving brother". While Washington was away from Mount Vernon during the French and Indian War he left the plantation in charge of this brother. They frequently visited each other, and during one of the darkest periods of the Revolutionary War, Washington wrote him as follows: "God grant you health and happiness. Nothing in this world would contribute so much to mine as to be with you." When John Augustine died in 1787, George Washington wrote in his diary his undisguised grief over the death of "my beloved brother". John Augustine married Hannah Bushrod; died at Bushfield on Nomini Creek, Westmoreland County, Virginia, in February, 1787, where he is buried. As will be seen elsewhere, George Washington provided in his will that Mount Vernon, after the death of Mrs. Washington, should descend to John Augustine's son, Bushrod Washington.

Childhood and Youth of Washington

Until he was about three years old, Washington resided with his parents at the ancestral home at Wakefield, when the family, "on account of sickness," took up their abode on the Epsewasson, or Hunting Creek estate, later called Mount Vernon, then in Prince William (now Fairfax) County. Here they dwelt until 1739, when they moved to the father's plantation called "Pine Grove" on the Rappahannock, where the father passed to eternal rest in April, 1743.

Upon the death of his father, Washington went to live with his half-brother Augustine, who had married the wealthy Ann Aylett and was now residing on the old homestead at Wakefield. After a time, he returned to his mother, who still resided, after the father's death, on the plantation on the Rappahannock. Later in the autumn of 1747, he came to Mount Vernon to reside with his other half-brother, Lawrence, now the owner of that estate, who had married Anne, daughter of William Fairfax. From this time Mount Vernon was his home. However, during his residence with his mother on the Rappahannock plantation, he made many extended visits to his half-brothers Augustine at Wakefield and Lawrence at Mount Vernon.

While residing with his half-brother Augustine at Wakefield, he attended a school several months in the year, kept near that place by a certain Williams; and while residing with his mother on the Rappahannock plantation, he attended a school at Fredericksburg, kept by the Reverend James Marye. His favorite study was mathematics. He learned surveying, became a licensed surveyor of Westmoreland County, and followed the profession for four years (1747-1751). During the year 1748 he assisted in the work of surveying the vast estates of Thomas, Lord Fairfax, which lay beyond the Blue Ridge Mountains in Virginia. His instructors in surveying were his half-brother Lawrence and his friend, George William Fairfax.

Historians almost universally make the statement that Washington never studied any language except English,

but there is in existence a copy of Patrick's Latin transla-
tion of Homer, printed in 1742, on the fly-leaf of which
is written, in a round schoolboy hand, the following:

> *"Hunc mihi quaeso (bone Vir) Libellum*
> *Redde si forsan tenues repertum*
> *Ut Scias qui sum sine fraude Scriptum,*
> *Est mihi nomen*

> GEORGIO WASHINGTON,
> GEORGE WASHINGTON,
> FREDERICKSBURG,
> VIRGINIA."

It would seem, therefore, that while attending
Reverend Marye's School at Fredericksburg, he must have
studied the elements of Latin.

As proofs of his diligence as a student, manuscripts
written by him in boyhood exhibit studies in geometry
and trigonometry. They are models of neatness. There
still exist, also, specimens of his ornamental penmanship
and fancy pen-sketch creations of birds. There is also in
existence a manuscript book of notes, bills of exchange,
bonds, deeds, etc., which he wrote at the age of thirteen to
familiarize himself with proper forms for transacting business.

But his studies as a boy were not all for the purpose of
acquiring intellectual attainments. He educated the heart
as well as the head. He collected and copied in one of his
manuscripts, "Rules of Behavior in Company and Con-
versation." Among these rules are the following:

> "Show not yourself glad at the misfortune of
> another, though he were your enemy."
> "Let your discourse with men of business be
> short and comprehensive."

"Wherein you reprove another, be unblamable yourself."

"Be not hasty to believe flying reports to the disparagement of any."

"In your apparel be modest, and endeavor to accommodate nature rather than to procure admiration."

"Associate yourself with men of good quality, if you esteem your own reputation."

"Speak not ill of the absent for it is unjust."

"Let your recreations be manful, not sinful."

"Labor to keep alive in your breast that little spark of celestial fire called Conscience."

These and similar maxims he made a part of himself. Among his favorite recreations as a boy were lifting and throwing heavy weights, jumping with a pole, and wrestling. He was also noted for his fleetness in running foot races with his school fellows, and tradition says he surpassed them all in this sport. It is also said that so great was the power of his right arm in youth that he would often throw a stone across the Rappahannock at the lower ferry of Fredericksburg—a wonderful feat. As a horseman, also, he was unsurpassed.

In 1746 an incident happened in the life of Washington which is worthy of notice from its important bearing on his future. We refer to his purpose to join the British navy. His half-brother Lawrence, at that time a member of the Virginia House of Burgesses and adjutant-general of his district, had served under Admiral Vernon and General Wentworth. A midshipman's warrant, obtained through Lawrence's influence, was put into the hands of the fourteen year old George, much to his delight. He made arrangements at once to embark on a man-of-war then riding in the Potomac, and his baggage was put on the ship. All that remained to be done before his departure was to receive the approbation and blessing of his mother. But the mother did not take kindly to the idea of having her son, so young in years, taken away from her, perhaps forever. Also her brother Joseph in London, whose counsel she sought, urgently advised her against the navy as a fit place for her son. She refused her consent to the separation from her, and George unmurmuringly yielded to his mother's wishes. Who will say that the Unseen was not present in the sympathies of that incident? He who controls the fates of men had a higher service in reserve for this noble boy.

As stated on page 30, George's half-brother, Lawrence, married Anne, eldest daughter of Hon. William Fairfax. The fine estate of Belvoir, five miles down the Potomac from Mount Vernon, was the Fairfax home. Hon. William Fairfax was a man of learning and culture. He had been Chief Justice of the Bahamas. The alliance of Lawrence with a daughter of such a person opened the way for George's acquaintance with the Fairfax family, and later his close friendship with William Fairfax's cousin, Thomas, the sixth Lord Fairfax, a man of education and great moral worth, a graduate of Oxford University.

Lord Fairfax was a man of wealth and had formerly moved in the best circles of English society; but having been disappointed in an affair of the heart, he sought seclusion in the forests of Virginia on the estates he had inherited from his mother. After coming to the colony he resided for some time with his cousin at Belvoir, enjoying its cultured atmosphere and participating with relish in the pastimes (mostly fox-hunting) of the local gentry. Later he took up his residence on a domain which he named "Greenway Court," in the Shennandoah Valley, thirteen miles south of Winchester, Virginia. Here he died shortly after he heard the news of the surrender of Cornwallis at Yorktown—tidings that hastened his end; for despite his friendship for Washington, he continued to the last hour of his life of ninety-two years, a loyal subject of the King. His last words were spoken to his body-servant: "Come, Joe, carry me to bed; for I'm sure 'tis high time for me to die." His body was deposited under the chancel of the Episcopal Church at Winchester.

When the young Washington first met Lord Fairfax, the latter had just come to Virginia, at the age of fifty-seven, to reside on his domain, and was at that time an inmate at Belvoir. In the Belvoir Mansion at that time, also, was Hon. William Fairfax's highly educated eldest son, George William, then about twenty-two years old, with his bride and her sister, accomplished daughters of Colonel Cary, of Virginia.

In almost daily society of such persons, young Washington enjoyed rare opportunities for intellectual growth and social culture. They appreciated his character, and he won their esteem. Lord Thomas especially became particularly attached to him. He and George were both fond of the chase, and were companions on many a fox hunt in the fields and forests of northern Virginia.

Beautiful Belvoir Mansion with its wide verandas was burned in the early part of the Revolution, and scarcely a brick remains to show where it stood. Hon. William Fairfax, the owner, and his wife, Deborah Clark, sleep in their graves in the edge of the forest near the location of their former home. Their son, George William, and his wife went to England just before the Revolution. Both died in the City of Bath, he in 1787 and she in 1811.

FAMOUS ATHENÆUM PORTRAIT OF WASHINGTON

By Gilbert Stuart

Stuart said that there were features in Washington's face totally different from
what he ever observed in the face of any other human being, the sockets for the eyes,
for instance, being larger than any he had ever seen before.

Washington carried throughout life the fondest recollections of his associations with the cultured family at Belvoir. After he returned to Mount Vernon at the close of the Revolution he wrote: "It is a matter of sore regret, when I cast my eyes towards Belvoir, which I often do, to reflect that the former inhabitants of it, with whom we lived in such harmony and friendship, no longer reside there, and that the ruins can only be viewed as the mementos of former pleasures."

The youthful Washington was not free from the throbbings of the tender passion. In one of his early manuscripts are found plaintive breathings of this nature, uttered for the relief of his "poor restless heart." The object of his attachment was a "Lowland beauty," but what her name was will likely remain a matter of speculation. Some authorities contend that she was Miss Betsy Fauntleroy; others, Miss Mary Bland; and others, Miss Lucy Grimes, who became the mother of General Henry Lee, the famous "Light Horse Harry" of the Revolution. He was also said to have been an admirer of Miss Sally Fairfax, but there were three Sally Fairfaxes. First, there was the wife of his friend George William Fairfax, who as Sally Cary, had married young Fairfax in 1748. Second, there was Sally (Sarah) Fairfax, daughter of Colonel William Fairfax, who married Major John Carlyle of Alexandria, while Washington was still attending school. Third, there was Sally Fairfax, daughter of Bryan, eldest son of Honorable William Fairfax. Though a pretty romance, the Sally Fairfax narrative is seen, under investigation, not to be plausible.

His name has also been connected with Miss Mary Cary, sister of the Sally Cary, who married George William Fairfax. He mentions both her and the "Lowland Beauty" in an undated letter to a certain "Dear Robin", evidently his cousin, Robert Washington, of Chotank:

> "My place or residence is at present at his lordships (Belvoir) where I might, was my heart disengaged, pass my time very pleasantly, as there's a very agreeable young lady in the same house (Mary Cary). But as that's only adding fuel to fire, it makes me the more uneasy, for by often and unavoidably being in company with her revives my former passion for your Lowland Beauty; whereas, was I to live more retired from young women, I might eleviate in some measure my sorrows by burying that chaste and troublesome passion in the grave of oblivion or eternal forgetfulness, for as I am very well assured, that's the only antidote or remedy that I ever shall be relieved by or only recess that can administer any cure or help to me, as I am well convinced, was I ever to attempt anything, I should only get a denial which would be only adding grief to uneasiness."

Many authorities believe the "Lowland Beauty" was Lucy Grimes, and if she actually was this lady, an explanation is thus afforded why Washington always regarded her famous son, "Light Horse Harry Lee", with such particular favor—the great Virginian, soldier, orator and member of Congress from Washington's Congressional district, who at the request of Congress, delivered the funeral oration on the death of Washington before that body assembled in the German Lutheran Church in Philadelphia on December 26, 1799, in which he declared him to be: "first in war, first in peace, and first in the hearts of his countrymen."—words that will thunder down the centuries until the end of time.

However, General Fitzhugh Lee, a great grandson of Lucy Grimes, believed that he satisfactorily identified the "Lowland Beauty" as Betsy Fauntleroy in his discovery of the following letter written by Washington to William Fauntleroy, Sr.:

"May 20, 1752.

"To Wm. Fauntleroy, Sr.

"Sir: I should have been down long before this, but my business in Frederick detained me somewhat longer than I expected and immediately upon my return from thence I was taken with a violent pleurice (pleurisy) which has reduced me very low; but purpose as soon as I recover my strength to wait on Miss Betsy in hopes of a revocation of the former cruel sentence, and see if I can meet with any alteration in my favor. I have enclosed a letter to her, which should be much obliged to you for the delivery of it. I have nothing to add but my best respts (respects) to your good lady and family.

GEORGE WASHINGTON."

Betsy Fauntleroy was the only daughter of William Fauntleroy whose plantation was at Naylor's Hold on the Rappahannock. She was born June 26, 1736.

Though the historian labors in vain to identify the "Lowland Beauty," her memory will dwell sweetly in the heart of the world, with that of her illustrious lover until time shall be no more.

Young George received military instruction. Two of his half-brother Lawrence's old comrades, Adjutant Muse and Jacob VanBraam, were employed by Lawrence to instruct the youthful Washington in the arts and artifices of war. Says Washington Irving in his classic "Life of Washington": "Under the tutelage of these veterans, Mount Vernon, from being a quiet rural retreat, where Washington, three years previously, had indited love ditties to his 'Lowland Beauty', was suddenly transformed into a school of arms, as he practiced the manual exercise with Adjutant Muse or took lessons on the broadsword from VanBraam."

The Young Surveyor

As stated on page 30, Washington assisted in the work of surveying the vast estates of Lord Fairfax in 1748. Accompanied by Hon. William Fairfax's son, George William, he set forth on this hazardous expedition in March, 1748, just after he entered upon his seventeenth year. They crossed the South Branch of the Potomac and the Allegheny mountains, and entered the Shennandoah Valley. The privations and experiences of this expedition he recorded in a journal written by him at the time. We quote the following extracts giving pictures of the scenes through which he passed:

"March 13th (1748). Rode to his lordship's quarter. About four miles higher up the river Shennandoah, we went through most beautiful groves of sugar-trees, and spent the best part of the day in admiring the trees, and the richness of the land.

"14th. We sent our baggage to Captain Hite's near Fredericktown, and went ourselves down the river about sixteen miles—the land exceedingly rich all the way, producing abundance of grain, hemp, and tobacco—in order to lay off some land on Cate's Marsh and Long Marsh.

"15th. Worked hard till night, and then returned. After supper we were lighted into a room; and I, not being so good a woodsman as the rest, stripped myself very orderly and went into the bed, as they called it, when, to my surprise, I found it to be nothing but a little straw matted together, without sheet or anything else but only one threadbare blanket, with double its weight of vermin. I was glad to get up and put on my clothes and lie as my companions did. Had we not been very tired, I am sure we should not have slept much that night. I made a promise to sleep so no more, choosing rather to sleep in the open air before a fire.

"18th. We traveled to Thomas Berwick's on the Potomac, where we found the river exceedingly high by reason of the great rains that had fallen among the Alleghenies. They told us it would not be fordable for several days, it being now six feet higher than usual, and rising. We agreed to stay till Monday. We this day called to see the famed Warm Springs. We camped out in the field this night.

"20th. Finding the river not much abated we in the evening swam our horses over to the Maryland side.

"21st. We went over in a canoe, and traveled up the Maryland side all day, in a continued rain, to Colonel Cresap's over against the mouth of the South Branch, about forty miles from our place of starting in the morning, and over the worst road, I believe, that ever was trod by man or beast.

"23rd. Rained till about 2 o'clock, and then cleared up, when we were agreeably surprised at the sight of more than thirty Indians coming from war, with only one scalp. We had some liquor with us, of which we gave them a part. This, elevating their spirits, put them in the humor of dancing. We then had a war dance. After clearing a

40

large space and making a great fire in the middle, the men seated themselves around it, and the speaker made a grand speech, telling them in what manner they were to dance. After he had finished, the best dancer jumped up as one awakened from sleep and ran and jumped about the ring in a most comical manner. He was followed by the rest. Then began their music, which was performed with a pot half full of water and a deerskin stretched tight over it, and a gourd with some shot in it to rattle, and a piece of horse's tail tied to it to make it look fine. One person kept rattling and another drumming all the while they were dancing.

"25th. Left Cresap's and went up the mouth of Patterson's creek. There we swam our horses over the Potomac, and went over ourselves in a canoe, and traveled fifteen miles, where we camped.

"26th. Traveled up to Solomon Hedge's, Esquire, one of his Majesty's Justices of the Peace in the county of Frederick, where we camped. When we came to supper, there was neither a knife on the table nor a fork, to eat with; but, as good luck would have it, we had knives of our own.

"28th. Traveled up the South Branch—having come to that river yesterday—about thirty miles to Mr. J. R.'s (horse-jockey), and about seventy miles from the mouth of the river.

"29th. This morning went out and surveyed 500 acres of land. Shot two wild turkeys.

"30th. Began our intended business of laying off lots.

"April 2d. A blowing, rainy night. Our straw, upon which we were lying, took fire; but I was luckily preserved by one of our men's awakening when it was in a flame. We have run off four lots this day.

"4th. This morning Mr. Fairfax left us with the in-

41

tention to go down to the mouth of the river. We surveyed two lots and were attended with a great company of people—men, women, and children—who followed us through the woods, showing their antic tricks. They would never speak English, but when spoken to they all spoke Dutch. This day our tent was blown down by the violence of the wind.

"6th. The last night was so intolerably smoky that we were obliged to leave our tent to the mercy of the wind and fire. Attended this day by the aforesaid company.

7th. This day one of our men killed a wild turkey that weighed twenty pounds. We surveyed 1,500 acres of land and returned to Vanmeter's about 1 o'clock. I took my horse and went up to see Mr. Fairfax. We slept in Cassey's house, which was the first night I had slept in a house since we came to the Branch.

"8th. We breakfasted at Cassey's and rode down to Vanmeter's to get our company together, which, when we had accomplished, we rode down below the Trough to lay off lots there. The Trough is a couple of ledges of mountains, impassable, running side by side for seven or eight miles and the river between them. You must ride round the back of the mountains to get below them. We camped in the woods and after we had pitched our tent and made a large fire, we pulled out our knapsack to recruit ourselves. Every one was his own cook. Our spits were forked sticks, our plates were large chips. As for dishes, we had none.

"10th. We took our farewell of the Branch and traveled over hills and mountains to Coddy's, on Great Cacapheon, about forty miles.

"12th. Mr. Fairfax got safe home; and I to my brother's house at Mount Vernon; which concludes my journal."

On July 20, 1749, Young Washington procured a commission from the president of William and Mary College appointing him a public surveyor of Westmoreland County. The original record of his appointment is still extant.

His experience as a surveyor in the forests and mountains of Virginia established his reputation as a youth of energy, ability and integrity. He might have lingered among the social pleasures of Mount Vernon and Belvoir, for his society was the delight of his half-brother, Lawrence, and he was always welcome at Belvoir; but he made the manly choice to fulfill the duties of his chosen occupation as a land surveyor—an employement that yielded him rich returns in developing his vigorous frame and acquainting him with the habits and opinions of the sturdy yeomanry of the backwoods. While making his surveys he frequently visited his old friend, Lord Fairfax, at "Greenway Court" and availed himself of the use of the latter's well-selected library.

Messenger to the French Forts

In 1753, Washington, then a Major in the Virginia militia, was sent by Governor Dinwiddie of Virginia to the commandant of the French Forts on the headwaters of the Allegheny river, bearing the governor's message demanding that the French withdraw their forces from the territory claimed by the English. This was a perilous journey through more than five hundred miles of wilderness among hostile Indians and in the dead of winter. Among his companions on this journey were his old fencing master, Van Braam, and Christopher Gist. Van-Braam acted as French interpreter, and Mr. Gist, an experienced scout and backwoodsman, as guide. On the return trip, Washington had two thrilling adventures

which are told in every school history of the United States
—the first when he was fired upon by an Indian, near the
present Evans City, Butler County, Pennsylvania,
and the second when he was almost drowned in the
Allegheny river within the present limits of Pittsburgh.
We quote the following extracts from his journal telling
in his own words the account of these adventures:

"The day following, December 27, 1753, just after we
had reached a place called Murdering Town (where we intended to quit the path and steer across the country for
Shannopin's Town), we fell in with a party of French Indians who had lain in wait for us. One of them fired at
Mr. Gist or me not fifteen steps off but fortunately missed.
We took this fellow into custody and kept him until about
9 o'clock at night, then let him go and walked all the remaining part of the night without making any stop that
we might get the start so far as to be out of the reach of
their pursuit the next day, since we were well assured they
would follow our track as soon as it was light. [A monument, long advocated by the author, now marks the ap-
proximate spot where the Indian attempted to kill Washington.]

"The next day we continued traveling until quite dark,
and got to the river (Allegheny) about two miles above
Shannopin's. We expected to find the river frozen, but it
was not, only about fifty yards from each shore. The ice,
I suppose, had broken up above for it was driving in vast
quantities.

"There was no way for getting over but on a raft which
we set about with but one poor hatchet and finished just
after sunsetting. This was a whole day's work; we next
got it launched then went on board of it and set off. But
before we were half way over we were jammed in the ice
in such a manner that we expected every moment our
raft to sink and ourselves to perish. I put out my setting

pole to try to stop the raft that the ice might pass by, when the rapidity of the stream threw it with so much violence against the pole that it jerked me out into ten feet of water, but I fortunately saved myself by catching hold of one of the raft logs. Notwithstanding all our efforts we could not get to either shore but were obliged as we were near an island to quit our raft and make to it.

"The cold was so extremely severe that Mr. Gist had all his fingers and some of his toes frozen, and the water was shut up so hard that we found no difficulty in getting off the island on the ice in the morning and went to Mr. Frazier's. We met here with twenty warriors who were going to the southward to war, but coming to a place on the head of the Great Kenhawa where they found seven people killed and scalped (all but one woman with very light hair), they turned about and ran back for fear the inhabitants would rise and take them as the authors of the murder. They report that the bodies were lying about the house and some of them much torn and eaten by the hogs. By the marks which were left they say they were French Indians of the Ottaway nation who did it.

"As we intended to take horses here and it required some time to find them, I went up about three miles to the mouth of the Youghiogheny to visit Queen Aliquippa, who had expressed great concern that we passed her in going to the fort. I made her a present of a matchcoat and a bottle of rum, which latter was thought much the better present of the two. [She was a Seneca Indian.]

"Tuesday, the 1st day of January, (1754), we left Mr. Frazier's house and arrived at Mr. Gist's, at Mononga-hela, the second, where I bought a horse and saddle. The sixth, we met seventeen horses loaded with materials and stores for a fort at the Fork of the Ohio, and the day after some families going out to settle. This day we arrived at Wills Creek, after as fatiguing a journey as it is possible to conceive, rendered so by excessive bad weather.

"From the first day of December to the fifteenth there was not one day on which it did not rain or snow incessantly, and throughout the whole journey we met with nothing but one continued series of cold, wet weather, which occasioned very uncomfortable lodgings, especially after we had quitted our tent, which was some screen from the inclemency of it.

On the eleventh, I got to Belvoir where I stopped one day to take necessary rest, and then set out and arrived in Williamsburg the sixteenth, where I waited upon his Honor the Governor, with the letter I had brought from the French commandant, and to give an account of the success of my proceedings."

This expedition was the foundation of Washington's fortunes. It showed him to be a youth of wonderful tact, sagacity, and self reliance. From now on, he was the rising hope of the Colony of Virginia.

Van Braam also accompanied Washington on the first campaign of the French and Indian War, and was the interpreter when Washington was compelled to surrender to the French at Fort Necessity, July 4, 1754, in the mountains near Uniontown, Pennsylvania—his first and only surrender. His limited knowledge of French in translating a certain word in the articles of capitulation as "death" instead of "assassination" laid Washington under the charge of having admitted that his force had "assassinated" Jumonville, the leader of the French, who was killed in the first engagement of that long and bloody war—a battle in which Washington is said to have fired the first gun. This engagement took place in an almost inaccessible rocky glen in the Allegheny mountains near Uniontown, Pennsylvania.

It not being the purpose of the author to write a complete biography of our principal subject, we now take leave of the youthful Washington.

Marriage and Household of Washington

Washington was married on January 6, 1759, to Martha Dandridge Custis, widow of Colonel Daniel Parke Custis, of York County, Virginia. Most histor-

Gen. Washington   Mrs. Washington
Geo. W. P. Custis   Nellie Custis   Wm. Lee

SAVAGE'S PICTURE OF THE WASHINGTON FAMILY

ians state that the marriage was solemnized at the "White House," the home of the bride on the Pamunky River in New Kent County, while others give St. Peter's Church, nearby, as the place of the nuptials. The first three months of their married life were spent at the "White House," after which they took up their residence at Mount Vernon.

Martha Washington was the daughter of Colonel

47

John Dandridge, of New Kent County, Virginia. She had married Daniel Parke Custis at the age of seventeen, and had been a widow a little over two years when she married Washington. She was the most wealthy woman in the Colony of Virginia, having a large landed estate and thirty thousand pounds sterling, together with numerous slaves.

Washington met his future wife when making a journey on military business to Williamsburg, the capital of the Colony of Virginia, in the spring of 1758. His biographer, Washington Irving, tells the story of this first meeting as follows:

"He set off promptly on horse-back attended by Bishop, the well-trained military servant, who had served the late General Braddock. It proved an eventful journey, though not in a military point of view. In crossing a ferry of the Pamunkey, a branch of the York River, he fell in company with a Mr. Chamberlayne, who lived in the neighborhood, and who, in the spirit of Virginian hospitality, claimed him as a guest. It was with difficulty Washington could be prevailed on to halt for dinner, so impatient was he to arrive at Williamsburg, and accomplish his mission.

"Among his guests at Mr. Chamberlayne's was a young and blooming widow, Mrs. Martha Custis, daughter of Mr. John Dandridge, both patrician names in the province. Her husband, John Parke Custis, had been dead about three years, leaving her with two young children, and a large fortune. She is represented as being rather below the middle size, but extremely well shaped, with an agreeable countenance, dark hazel eyes and hair, and those frank, engaging manners, so captivating in Southern women. We are not informed whether Washington had met with her before; probably not during her widow-

48

hood, as during that time he had been almost continually on the frontier.

"It was not until the next morning that he was again in the saddle, spurring for Williamsburg. Happily the White House, the residence of Mrs. Custis, was in New Kent County, at no great distance from that city, so that he had opportunities of visiting her in the intervals of business."

On July 20, 1758, when on his way to join the army of General Forbes, which was advancing against the French at Fort Duquesne, he wrote the following love letter to Mrs. Custis from Fort Cumberland:

"To Martha Custis:

"We have begun our march for the Ohio. A courier is starting for Williamsburg, and I embrace the opportunity to send a few words to one whose life is now inseparable from mine. Since that happy hour when we made our pledges to each other, my thoughts have been continually going to you as to another self. That an All Powerful Providence may keep us both in safety is the prayer of your ever faithful and ever affectionate friend,

G. Washington."

Mrs. Custis was the mother of four children: Frances, Daniel, John Parke and Martha Parke, "Patsy", as she was affectionately called. Only John Parke and "Patsy" were living at the time of their mother's marriage to Washington. Frances and Daniel had died young, and were first buried in Marsden Cemetery near the White House. Later their bodies were removed to Bruton Churchyard in Williamsburg. John Parke and "Patsy" were brought to Mount Vernon, and Washington became their guardian.

"Patsy" was a delicate child. As she grew to girlhood she developed epilepsy. In 1769 Washington took her over the mountains to the "Warm Springs" in the hope that she might receive benefit from the health-giving waters. He sadly notes in his diary that she received "little benefit." After four years more of suffering she died June 19, 1773, and with marble face upturned to the glorious summer sky, was laid away from sight in the tomb at Mount Vernon until the heavens be no more. Then Washington wrote with a heavy heart: "The Sweet Innocent Girl entered into a more happy and peaceful abode than she has met with in the afflicted path she has hitherto trod. It is an easier matter to conceive than to describe the distress of this family over the death of dear 'Patsy' Custis."

John Parke Custis was tutored by the Reverend Mr. Boucher, and, for some time attended King's College (now Columbia), in New York City. While pursuing his studies he had become deeply enamored of Eleanor, second daughter of Benedict Calvert, (a descendant of Lord Baltimore) of Mount Airy, Maryland, to whom he was married on February 3, 1774. Mrs. Washington, still deeply grieving over the death of "Patsy", was unable to attend her son's wedding, but wrote her new daughter as follows:

"My dear Nelly: God took from me a daughter, when June roses were blooming—he has now given me another daughter, about her age when winter winds are blowing, to warm my heart again. I am as happy as one so afflicted and so blest can be. Pray receive my benediction

and a wish that you may long live the loving
wife of my happy son, and a loving daughter of   ,
Your affectionate mother,

M. WASHINGTON."

Young Custis and his bride resided at Mount Vernon
for about two years. Then they moved to Abingdon,
their beautiful estate on the Potomac above Alexandria.
During the Revolution, Mr. Custis became an officer in
the Virginia militia, and was an aide to Washington during the siege of Yorktown. He contracted camp fever
during the siege, and was removed to Eltham, the residence of Mrs. Washington's sister in New Kent County,
at which place he died on November 5, 1781, aged twenty-
seven years. He is buried at Eltham.

John Parke Custis was survived by his widow and
four small children: Eliza, born August 21, 1776;
Martha, born December 31, 1777; Eleanor, born March
21, 1779; and George Washington Parke, born April 30,
1781. The two younger, Eleanor and George Washington
Parke, were adopted by Washington, upon the death of
their father, and reared in his household at Mount Vernon.
Eliza (Elizabeth) and Martha not having been part of
the household at Mount Vernon, we shall not trace their
history further than to state that Eliza became the wife of
Mr. Thomas Law and Martha married Mr. Thomas Peter.

Eleanor (Nellie) Custis became a lady of rare charm of
manner and beauty of person. She was a great favorite
of her grandmother and her foster father. She shed much
sunlight in the Mount Vernon home. When she attained
marriageable age, she had many suitors, among them being a son of Charles Carroll, of Carrollton, Maryland; but
George Washington's nephew, Lawrence Lewis, son of
Betty Washington and Colonel Fielding Lewis, of Fred-

ericksburg, was the favored one. He had made many visits to Mount Vernon, and in the latter years of Washington's life, had been invited by his uncle to make that place his home. On Washington's birthday, 1799, the last birthday that was ever to dawn on Washington, Nellie and Lawrence were married at Mount Vernon. That night Washington recorded the event in his diary: "Miss Custis was married about candle light to Mr. Lawrence Lewis."

Nellie and Lawrence resided at Mount Vernon until after the death of Mrs. Washington, when they removed to a tract of land consisting of about two thousand acres, a part of the Mount Vernon estate, given to Lewis by George Washington in his will. Here in 1804, Lawrence erected on this tract, on a site selected originally by the General, one of the most imposing homes in that part of Virginia which he named "Woodlawn." Tradition says that Washington designed the stately structure.

For nearly forty years, Nelly was mistress of "Woodlawn." Here her four children were born: Agnes, the eldest, dying at school in Philadelphia; Frances Parke, who married General E. G. W. Butler; Lorenzo, her only son; and Eleanor Angela, who married Hon. C. M. Conrad, of Louisiana.

On November 20, 1839, Major Lawrence Lewis died at Arlington, and his body was laid away in the tomb at Mount Vernon. After his death Nellie moved to "Audley", one of her husband's estates, near Berryville, in Clarke County, Virginia. Here she died July 15, 1852, and her body was brought to Mount Vernon and buried beside the tomb wherein lie the bodies of her foster-parent, her grandmother, and her husband.

W. H. Snowden, in his excellent work, "Some Old Historic Land Marks of Virginia and Maryland", thus describes the long journey of "Nellie Custis" back to Mount Vernon to sleep the last long sleep amid its hallowed associations:

"To the watcher from farm house and village, that must have been a lonely and mournful funeral procession indeed, as it slowly wended its course down the long Virginia highway from the Shennandoah to the Potomac. The hearse containing the remains of the aged grandmother, and a solitary carriage accompanying, with the two surviving grandsons, one of whom was lately living to tell of the impressive circumstances of the event. Late at night their journey was finished, and the coffined form of Nelly was placed in the parlor at Mount Vernon, where, more than fifty years before, crowned with bridal wreaths, the 'fairest lady of the land,' Washington himself had affectionately given her in marriage, and commended her to the protecting care of the one favored claimant of her choice, and where she had received the congratulations and blessings of so many of her kinsfolk and friends. Many of the citizens of Alexandria and Washington and the surrounding country came to pay their tributes of fond remembrance and regard to 'Nelly' as she lay in state in the 'Mansion', and to see the last of 'earth to earth.'

Down in the family burial place, just by the waters of the river on whose pleasant banks she had passed so many happy days of childhood and youth, her dust is very near to that of her kind and loving guardians. A marble monument marks her last resting place with the following inscription:

"SACRED

TO THE MEMORY OF ELEANOR PARKE CUSTIS, GRANDDAUGHTER OF MRS. WASHINGTON, AND ADOPTED DAUGHTER OF GENERAL WASHINGTON.

"Reared under the roof of the Father of his Country, this lady was not more remarkable for the beauty of her person than for the superiority of her mind. She lived to be admired, and died to be regretted, July 15, 1852, in the seventy-fourth year of her age."

George Washington Parke Custis was taught by private tutors at Mount Vernon, and later attended the College of New Jersey (Princeton), the College of Philadelphia, and Annapolis. In 1804, he married Miss Mary Lee Fitzhugh, daughter of William Fitzhugh of Chatham, Stafford County. Chatham Mansion is still standing opposite Fredericksburg. He inherited Arlington where he lived until his death, October 10th, 1857, and is buried by the side of his wife on the slopes of that beautiful estate, now the Arlington National Cemetery.

Reared under the roof of the "Father of His Country," he enjoyed the advantages of the cultured society and companionship of this home. In later years he became a writer and orator of ability. He wrote a biography of the General, called "Recollections of Washington," which carries the reader into the inner circle of the home at Mount Vernon. On June 30, 1831, his only surviving child, Mary Ann Randolph Custis, was married at Arlington House to Robert E. Lee, son of the famous "Light Horse Harry" and grandson of Lucy Grimes, the probable "Lowland Beauty" of Washington's early love.

Early History of Mount Vernon

The history of "Mount Vernon on the Potomac" goes back to 1674 in which year Thomas, Lord Culpepper conveyed to George Washington's great-grandfather, John Washington, the Immigrant, and Nicholas Spencer 5000 acres of land situated on the Potomac River between

Epsewasson (as Dogue Creek and neighborhood were called in the language of the Indians who roamed the hills and vales of this region) and Little Hunting Creeks. The consideration of the grant was services rendered the Colony of Virginia by Washington and Spencer in bringing one hundred immigrants into its virgin wilds.

John Washington, upon his death in 1677, devised his share in the tract to his son Lawrence, the grandfather of George. In 1690, a division of the tract was made by which Lawrence received 2500 acres lying to the north and east on the Potomac and Hunting Creek.

Lawrence Washington, upon his death in 1698, devised his half of the tract, thus set apart, to his daughter Mildred, describing it in his will as "all my land in Stafford County, lying upon Hunting Creek . . . by estimation 2500 acres."

Mildred married Roger Gregory, and she and her husband conveyed the tract to her brother Augustine Washington, George's father, by deed of May 26, 1726, for the consideration of one hundred and eighty pounds.

Augustine and his family resided on the estate from 1735 to the latter part of 1739. During this period, he built a grist mill on the banks of the Epsewasson (Dogue Run) two miles west of the Mansion, which was in continuous operation for more than one hundred years. It was built on a 200 acre tract which Augustine added to the estate by purchase from the heirs of Nicholas Spencer. Some portions of the foundation are still intact, and marks of the mill race can be traced.

William H. Snowden, in "Some Old Historical Landmarks of Virginia and Maryland," pays the following beautiful tribute to Washington's mill:

"But go there, reader, as the writer has gone many a time, if your sympathies and reverential inclinations are for objects like these, and take your seat in the drowsy quiet of a midsummer day under the shadowy branches of one of the oaks still remaining of the olden forest; and while you gaze on the briar grown ruins and listen to the murmur of the dwindled stream which goes hurrying on in its course to join the waters of the majestic bay but a mile or two beyond, the mystic veil which hides the vanished years of a century and a half will rise, and lo! all around you will throng the faded scenes and forms of the early days. The fallen stones will move from the scattered heaps under the straggling vines and brambles and take their places in the walls again. The mill of Augustine and George Washington will be itself once more. The water will come pouring down over the mossy wheel. You will hear the clattering of the grinding gear, and the plantation swains will bring in and carry away their burdens.

"You will see the dusty miller taking his tolls and filling the bin. A horseman will ride up, and hitching his steed by the door, go in and hold parley with the miller, and you will not need to ask who he is, for his stately mien and dignified bearing will at once proclaim him the proprietor. You will see, too, the trading schooner waiting at the landing for its cargo for Jamaico or Barbadoes. The early pioneers in rough home-spun garb and quaint vehicles will pass along the old highway by you in toilsome march for the new Canaan of their imaginations, there to fix their landmarks and lay the hearthstones. Anon, you will see straggling companies of provincial troops dressed in kersey or buckskin, with heavy flint lock muskets on their shoulders, hurrying up to the camp at the new born hamlet of Alexandria. General Braddock and Governor Dinwiddie, Commodore Kepple and General St. Clair will ride along in the pomp and viceregal chariot and dashing retinue and guards of British regulars in showy scarlet uniforms and bright with gilding and tinsel. War's wild alarm has been sounded, and the frontiers must be held against the encroachments of the French and their murderous Indian allies.

"Among other passers up the highway you will see a stripling wagon boy in homely workman's garb driving his own team, and like the rest of the wayfarers hurrying to the camp. He has been for years in the employ of John Ballandine, hauling iron ore to his furnace at Colchester, but the drum and fife of the troopers and the wild rumors of war have opened the vision of his adventurous spirit to other duties and other lines of action. He is going to offer his team to Braddock's quartermaster to haul supplies for the army over the mountains. Very obscure, lowly and friendless was this wagon boy then, but under that homespun shirt and buckskin cap were the lion heart and comprehensive intellect which when, ere long, the opportunities came to him, were to win for him a renown as a soldier and commander, world wide and imperishable.

"The boy who plodded over the weary roads of the Occoquan with his loads of ore for the furnace became in after years the strategic and trusted soldier, the intrepid leader of the riflemen of Virginia and the swaying spirit and hero of Quebec, Saratoga and Cowpens—Daniel Morgan."

It is highly probable that Augustine built the old brick barn still standing near the present Mansion house, though some claim that it was erected by his son Lawrence. He also built the first house on the estate, but the exact location of this hallowed fireside about which the parents of our Washington listened to the childish prattle of their immortal son will most likely remain forever unknown. Some place it in the vicinity

MARTHA WASHINGTON
Died at Mount Vernon on May 22, 1802. Her body rests beside that of George Washington in the vestibule, in front of the new tomb at Mount Vernon.

58

of the grist mill on the Epsewasson, while others believe it near or on the exact location of the present Mansion. But, wherever it stood, it was burned in 1739, whereupon Augustine and his family moved to his estate on the Rappahannock. It is also highly probable that Augustine, and not his son Lawrence, erected the middle part of the present Mansion at Mount Vernon as a residence for Lawrence, as maintained by Mr. Charles H. Callahan in his volume on Washington.

Augustine granted the estate, enlarged by above purchase, to his son Lawrence in 1740, and later confirmed the grant in his will in 1743, with reversion to his son George, "in Case my son Lawrence should dye without heirs of his body Lawfully begotten."

As stated elsewhere, it was Lawrence who named the estate "Mount Vernon" in honor of his old commander, Admiral Vernon. When Lawrence died in July, 1752, he devised Mount Vernon to his wife, Anne, for the term of her natural life, and, at her death, to his daughter, Sarah, with the provision that, should Sarah die without issue, the estate should descend "unto my loving brother George Washington." Sarah was less than one year old at the time of her father's death, and she survived him only a few months. Anne, the widow of Lawrence, on December 16, 1752, married Mr. George Lee, and shortly thereafter, she and her husband conveyed her life interest to Gorge Washington, who, thus, at the age of twenty completed his title to the estate.

Later History of Mount Vernon

Washington added to the estate by purchase until, in the latter years of his life, it was a plantation of over eight thousand acres with more than three thousand acres under cultivation. In order that it might be efficiently managed, he divided the plantation into five parts, called "Mansion House Farm," "River Farm," "Union Farm," "Muddy Hole Farm" and "Dogue Run Farm." Each of these farms had an overseer to manage it, who sent weekly reports to Washington when he was away from home.

The General took great pride in his mill on the banks of the Epsewasson, which, it will be recalled, was built by his father. He said that the flour which he made there was of such "superior quality that it passed in English markets without inspection."

He beautified the grounds about the Mansion, and twice enlarged it, first in 1760 and again in 1785. The banquet hall at one end and library at the other were the additions made, together with another story to the whole.

During the Revolution, Mrs. Washington spent nearly half of the time with the General at the front; and at such times Mount Vernon was almost deserted. The mansion was quiet; the woods no longer echoed to the hounds and horn of the huntsman. However, the work of tilling the plantation went on under the supervision of Lund Washington, a distant relative of the General; and Washington directed him, as follows, in a letter written from Cambridge: "Let the hospitality of the house, with respect to the poor be kept up. Let no one go away hungry. If any of this kind of people should be in want of corn, supply their necessities, provided it does not encourage them in idleness; and I have no objection to you giving my money in charity, to the amount of forty or fifty pounds a year, when you think it well bestowed."

During the Revolution there were several alarms at Mount Vernon caused by rumors that British ships and troops were on their way to destroy the plantation; and although at one time, warships actually anchored off the Mansion, no damage was done by them.

Washington loved Mount Vernon with a passionate love, and how his soul must have yearned for the restful home during his longest absence from it, that of six years, while fighting the battles of the Revolutionary War. He called it his "vine and fig tree," his "goal of domestic enjoyment." "I had rather be at Mount Vernon with a friend or two about me," he said, "than to be attended at the seat of government by the officers of state and the representatives of every power in Europe."

The following extracts from letters of Washington show his love for Mount Vernon:

In September, 1759, he wrote to Richard Washington, a relative in London, England: "I am now, I believe, fixed at this seat (Mount Vernon) with an agreeable consort for life; and hope to find more happiness in retirement than I ever experienced amidst a wide and bustling world."

Again, he speaks of Mount Vernon in strong terms of praise in a letter to Arthur Young, the celebrated English farmer, in 1793: "No estate in United America is more pleasantly situated than this. It lies in a high, dry, and healthful country three hundred miles by water from the sea, and, as you will see by the plan, on one of the finest rivers in the world. Its margin is washed by more than ten miles of tide-water, from the bed of which and the innumerable coves, inlets, and small marshes with which it abounds, an inexhaustible fund of rich mud may be drawn as manure, either to be used separately or in a compost, according to the judgment of the farmer. It is situated in a latitude between the extremes of heat and cold, and is the same distance by land and water with good roads and the best navigation to and from the Federal City, Alexandria and Georgetown, distant from the first twelve, from the second, nine, and from the last sixteen miles. This river which encompasses the land the distance above mentioned, is well supplied with various kinds of fish at all seasons of the year, and in the spring, with the greatest profusion of shad, herring, bass, carp, perch, sturgeon, etc. Several fisheries appertain to the estate; the whole shore, in short, is one entire fishery."

And to the Marchioness de Lafayette, he wrote as follows:

"From the clangor of arms and the bustle of a camp, freed from the cares of public employment and the responsibility of office, I am now enjoying domestic ease under the shadow of my own vine and fig tree; and in a small villa, with the implements of husbandry and lambkins around me, I expect to glide gently down the stream of life, till I am entombed in the dreary mansion of my fathers."

The eminent English writer, Charles Varlo, visited Washington in 1784, and has given the following interesting description of the life at Mount Vernon at that period:

"I crossed the river from Maryland into Virginia, near to the renowned General Washington's, where I had the honor to spend some time and was kindly entertained with that worthy family. As to the General, if we may judge by the countenance, he is what the world says of him, a shrewd, good natured, plain human man, about fifty-five years of age, and seems to wear well, being healthful and active, straight, well-made and about six feet high. He keeps a good table, which is always open to those of a genteel appearance. He does not use many Frenchified congees, or flattering useless words without meaning, which savor more of deceit than an honest heart, but on the contrary, his words seem to point at truth and reason, and to spring from the fountain of a heart, which being good of itself, cannot be suspicious of others.

"The General's house is rather warm, snug, convenient and useful than ornamental. The size is what ought to suit a man of about two or three thousand a year in England. The out-offices are good, and seem to be not long built and he was making more offices at each wing, to the front of the house, which added more to ornament than real use. The situation is high, and commands a beautiful prospect of the river which parts Virginia and Maryland, but in other respects the situation seems to be out of the world, being chiefly surrounded by woods, and far from any great road or thoroughfare, and nine miles from Alexandria, in Virginia. The General's lady is a hearty, comely, discreet, affable woman, some few years * older than himself; she was a widow when he married her. He has no children by her. The General's house is open to poor travelers as well as rich. He gives diet and lodging to all that come that way.

"I have traveled and seen a great deal of the world, have conversed with all degrees of people, and have remarked that there are only two persons in the world which have everyone's good word, and those are—the Queen of England and General Washington, which I never heard friend or foe speak lightly of."

When the Revolutionary General closed his eyes forever on the familiar scenes of Mount Vernon, he devised that part of the estate on which the Mansion is located, consisting of 4000 acres, to his favorite nephew, Bushrod Washington, son of his brother, John Augustine, and at that time one of the justices of the Supreme Court of the United States. Bushrod came into possession at the

* Mrs. Washington was three months younger than the General.

63

JUDGE BUSHROD WASHINGTON .

to whom the General willed Mount Vernon Mansion and surrounding four thousand acres of land. Bushrod Washington
was the General's favorite nephew, the son of his brother, John
Augustine. Judge Washington was one of the Justices of the
Supreme Court of the United States, having been appointed to
this high office by President John Adams in 1798. He was
one of the greatest Nisi Prius judges our country has had.
Died while attending court in Philadelphia, November 26, 1829,
aged sixty-seven years. Buried in the tomb at Mount Vernon.

death of Martha Washington, which occurred on May 22, 1802.

Judge Bushrod Washington left no children, and upon his death on November 26, 1829, he devised the Mansion and about 1225 acres of the adjoining land to his nephew, John A. Washington.

John A. Washington, above named, died on June 16, 1832, and devised his entire estate to his wife, Mrs. Jane C. Washington; and she granted Mount Vernon to her son John A. Washington, by deed dated September 18, 1849. Mrs. Jane Washington died in 1855, and confirmed the deed to her son in her will.

This John A. Washington was the last private owner of Mount Vernon. After offering Mount Vernon both to the State of Virginia and the United States, on their own terms, which offers were unaccepted, he sold the Mansion and about 200 acres of the adjoining land to the Mount Vernon Ladies' Association of the Union, formal possession being given February 22, 1860.

The last private owner of Mount Vernon, was a man of noble nature. Tempting offers were made him by speculators for the purchase of the estate, but he firmly rejected them. He was offered three hundred thousand dollars for the property he sold to the Mount Vernon Ladies' Association of the Union for two hundred thousand dollars.

At the beginning of the Civil War, Mr. Washington threw his fortunes with his native state. He became an aide with the rank of colonel on the staff of General Robert E. Lee, and was killed in the engagement at Cheat Mountain, in what is now West Virginia, on September 13, 1861.

The privilege of visiting the home of the Father of His Country and the satisfaction of knowing that it is to be preserved as a national shrine for all time, we owe to the Mount Vernon Ladies' Association of the Union, and beyond it, to that noble daughter of the Southland, Miss Ann Pamela Cunningham, whose high resolve and untiring labors brought the Ladies' Association into being. And let us not forget the aid given the Association, in the days of its early struggles, by the great American orator, Edward Everett, who turned over to its treasury the proceeds of his lecture on Washington, in the sum of almost seventy thousand dollars. Hear his eloquent words on Mount Vernon:

> "There is a modest private mansion on the banks of the Potomac, the abode of George Washington and Martha, his beloved, his loving, his faithful wife. It boasts no spacious palace or gorgeous colonnades, no massive elevation or storied tower. . . . No arch nor column in courtly English or courtlier Latin sets forth the deeds or worth of the Father of His Country. He needs them not. The unwritten benedictions of millions cover all the walls. No gilded dome swells from the lowly roof to catch the morning or evening beam, but the love and gratitude of united America settle upon it in one eternal sunshine. From beneath that humble roof went forth the intrepid, unselfish warrior, the magistrate who knew no glory but his country's good; to that he returned, happiest when his work was done. There he lived in noble simplicity; there he died in glory and peace. While it stands, the latest generations of the grateful children of America will make this pilgrimage to it as to a shrine; and when it shall fall, if fall it must, the memory and the name of Washington shall shed an eternal glory on the spot."

Last Days at Mount Vernon

"We arrived here on Wednesday, March 15th, without any accidents, after a tedious and fatiguing journey of seven days. Grandpa is very well and much pleased with being once more farmer Washington." Thus wrote Nellie Custis from Mount Vernon to a friend in Philadelphia, upon Washington's arrival at Mount Vernon, in the spring of 1797, to spend the remainder of his days on his plantation, after his abundant labors as President of the United States. And farmer once more he became. His long loved Mount Vernon absorbed his attention more and more, and public life receded farther into the background of his memory. He daily rode to the extremities of the estate and stopped frequently at his grist mill on the banks of the Epsewasson. How the time passed with him, he tells in a letter to James McHenry, Secretary of War, May 29, 1797:

"I begin my diurnal course with the sun. If my hirelings are not in their place at that time, I send them messages expressive of my sorrow at their indisposition. Having put these wheels in motion, I examine the state of things further, and the more they are probed, the deeper I find the wounds are which my buildings have sustained by an absence and neglect of eight years. By the time I have accomplished these matters, breakfast (a little after seven o'clock), is ready. This being over, I mount my horse and ride round my farms, which employs me until it is time to dress for dinner, at which I rarely miss seeing strange faces, come, as they say, out of respect for me. Pray, would not the word curiosity answer as well? The usual time of sitting at table, a walk, and tea, brings me within the dawn of candle-light, previous to which, if not prevented by company, I resolve that, as soon as the glimmering taper supplies the place of the great luminary, I will retire to my writing table and acknowledge the letters I have received; but when the lights are brought, I feel tired and disinclined to engage in this work, conceiving that the next night will do as well. The next comes, and with it the same causes for postponement, and effect, and so on."

In the above quoted letter he further states that he does not have as much time as he would like for reading, and that probably "before the nights grow longer," he may "be looking in Doomsday-Book."

His house was constantly filled with guests of all classes, yet he made the daily round of his farms. His correspondence, too, was very great, necessitating the employment of two secretaries to assist in this work, and also to copy and catalogue the enormous accumulation of his private and public papers.

When war with France was threatened in 1798, and President Adams appointed Washington Commander-in-Chief of all the armies to be raised, he accepted the command with the distinct understanding that he was not to be called from Mount Vernon for active service until hostilities made it absolutely necessary for him to take the field.

November, 1799, was a month of expectation and preparation in the Mount Vernon home, and on the 27th, the first child of Washington's nephew, Lawrence Lewis and his wife Nellie Custis, a daughter, was born in the Mansion.

Early in December of the same year, Washington pointed out to Lawrence Lewis the spot where he intended to build a new vault to replace the old one which he had built shortly after the death of his half-brother, Lawrence, and to which he had removed Lawrence's body from the old burial ground on the estate. He remarked to Lawrence Lewis that the building of a new tomb would be the next improvement that he would make, adding, "for after all I may require it before the rest." These prophetic words were soon to be fulfilled.

Last Hours of Washington

Washington continued his custom of daily visits to his various farms until two days before his death. On Thursday, December 12, 1799, he was caught in a storm of snow and rain, while visiting his farms, and the exposure caused an inflammation of the throat, from which he died on Saturday evening, December 14th.

His secretary, Mr. Tobias Lear, thus records the last hours of the Father of His Country:

Mount Vernon, Saturday, December 14th, 1799.

"This day being marked by an event, which will be memorable in the history of America and perhaps of the world, I shall give a particular statement of it, to which I was an eye-witness.

"On Thursday, December 12th, the General rode out to his farms about ten o'clock, and did not return home till past three. Soon after he went out, the weather became very bad, rain, hail, snow falling alternately, with a cold wind. When he came in, I carried some letters to

FRONT VIEW OF MOUNT VERNON MANSION

From an old picture. This more nearly represents the mansion and grounds as they appeared in the latter days of

him to frank, intending to send them to the postoffice in the evening. He franked the letters, but said the weather was too bad to send a servant to the office that evening. I observed to him, that I was afraid he had got wet. He said, No, his great-coat had kept him dry. But his neck appeared to be wet, and the snow was hanging upon his hair. He came to dinner (which had been waiting for him) without changing his dress. In the evening he appeared as well as usual.

"A heavy fall of snow took place on Friday, which prevented the General from riding out as usual. He had taken cold, undoubtedly from being so much exposed the day before, and complained of a sore throat. He, however, went out in the afternoon into the ground between the house and the river to mark some trees, which were to be cut down in the improvement of that spot. He had a hoarseness, which increased in the evening; but he made light of it.

"In the evening the papers were brought from the post office, and he sat in the parlor with Mrs. Washington and myself reading them, till about nine o'clock, when Mrs. Washington went into Mrs. Lewis' room, who was confined, and left the General and myself reading the papers. He was very cheerful, and when he met with anything interesting or entertaining he read it aloud as well as his hoarseness would permit. He requested me to read to him the debates of the Virginia Assembly, on the election of a Senator and Governor; and, on hearing Mr. Madison's observations respecting Mr. Monroe, he appeared much affected and spoke with some degree of asperity on the subject, which I endeavored to moderate, as I always did on such occasions. On his retiring I observed to him, he had better take something to remove his cold. He answered, 'No, you know I never take anything for a cold. Let it go as it came.'

"Between two and three o'clock on Saturday morning, he awoke Mrs. Washington, and told her that he was very unwell, and he had had an ague. She observed that he could scarcely speak, and breathed with difficulty, and would have got up to call a servant. But he would not permit her, lest she should take a cold. As soon as the day appeared, the woman (Caroline) went into the room to make a fire and Mrs. Washington sent her immediately to call me. I got up, put on my clothes as quickly as possible, and went to his chamber. Mrs. Washington was then up, and related to me his being ill as before stated. I found the General breathing with difficulty, and hardly able to utter a word intelligibly. He desired Mr. Rawlins (one of the overseers) might be sent for to bleed him before the doctor could arrive. I despatched a servant instantly for Rawlins, and another for Dr. Craik, and returned again to the General's chamber, where I found him in the same situation as I had left him.

"A mixture of molasses, vinegar and butter was prepared to try its effects on the throat; but he could not swallow a drop. Whenever he attempted it, he appeared to be distressed, convulsed, and almost suffocated. Rawlins came in soon after sunrise, and prepared to bleed him. When the arm was ready, the General observed that Rawlins appeared to be agitated, said, as well as he could speak, 'Don't be afraid.' And when the incision was made, he observed, 'The orifice is not large enough.' However, the blood ran pretty freely. Mrs. Washington, not knowing whether bleeding was proper or not in the General's situation, begged that much might not be taken from him, lest it should be injurious, and desired me to stop it; but when I was about to untie the string, the General put up his hand to prevent it, and, as soon as he could speak, he said, 'More, more.' Mrs. Washington being still very uneasy lest too much blood should be taken, it was stopped after taking about half a pint. Finding that no relief was obtained from bleeding, and that nothing would go down the throat, I proposed bathing it externally with sal volatile, which was done, and in the operation, which was with the hand, and in the gentlest manner, he observed, 'It is very sore.' A piece of flannel dipped in sal volatile was put around his neck, and his feet bathed in warm water, but without affording any relief.

"In the meantime, before Dr. Craik arrived, Mrs. Washington desired me to send for Dr. Brown, of Port Tobacco, whom Dr. Craik had recommended to be called, if any case should ever occur, that was seriously alarming. I despatched a messenger immediately for Dr. Brown, between eight and nine o'clock. Dr. Craik came in soon after, and, upon examining the General, he put a blister of cantharides on the throat, took some more blood from him, and had a gargle of vinegar and sage tea prepared; and ordered some vinegar and hot water for him to inhale the steam of it, which he did; but in attempting to use the gargle he was almost suffocated. When the gargle came from the throat, some phlegm followed, and he attempted to cough, which the doctor encouraged him to do as much as possible; but he could only attempt it. About eleven o'clock Dr. Craik requested that Dr. Dick might be sent for, as he feared Dr. Brown would not come in time. A messenger was accordingly despatched for him. About this time the General was bled again. No effect, however, was procured by it, and he remained in the same state, unable to swallow anything.

"Dr. Dick came about three o'clock and Dr. Brown arrived soon after. Upon Dr. Dick's seeing the General, and consulting a few minutes with Dr. Craik, he was bled again. The blood came very slow, was thick, and did

MOUNT VERNON MANSION

not produce any symptoms of fainting. Dr. Brown came into the chamber soon after, and upon feeling the General's pulse, the physicians went out together. Dr. Craik returned soon after. The General could now swallow a little. Calomel and tartar were administered, but without any effect.

"About half past four o'clock he desired me to call Mrs. Washington to his bedside, when he requested her to go down into his room, and take from his desk two wills, which she would find there, and bring them to him, which she did. Upon looking at them he gave her one, which he observed was useless, as being superseded by the other, and desired her to burn it, which she did, and took the other and put it into her closet.

"After this was done, I returned to his bedside and took his hand. He said to me: 'I find I am going. My breath cannot last long. I believed from the first that the disorder would prove fatal. Do you arrange and record all my late military letters and papers. Arrange my accounts and settle my books as you know more about them than anyone else, and let Mr. Rawlins finish recording my other letters, which he had begun.' I told him this should be done. He then asked, if I recollected anything which it was essential for him to do, as he had but a very short time to continue with us. I told him, that I could recollect nothing but that I hoped he was not so near his end. He observed, smiling, that he certainly was, and that, as it was the debt which we must all pay, he looked to the event with perfect resignation.

"In the course of the afternoon he appeared to be in great pain and distress, from the difficulty of breathing, and frequently changed his posture in the bed. On these occasions I lay upon the bed and endeavored to raise him and turn him with as much ease as possible. He appeared penetrated with gratitude for my attentions, and often said, 'I am afraid I shall fatigue you too much,' and upon assuring him, that I could feel nothing but a wish to give him ease, he replied, 'Well, it is a debt we must pay to each other, and I hope when you want aid of this kind, you will find it.'

"He asked when Mr. Lewis and Washington Custis would return. (They were then in New Kent.) I told him about the 20th of the month.

"About five o'clock Dr. Craik came again into the room, and, upon going to the bedside the General said to him, 'Doctor, I die hard, but I am not afraid to go. I believed, from my first attack, that I should not survive it. My breath cannot last long.' The doctor pressed his hand, but could not utter a word. He retired from the bedside, and sat by the fire absorbed in grief.

"Between five and six o'clock Dr. Dick and Dr. Brown came into the room, and with Dr. Craik went to the bed, when Dr. Craik asked him if he could sit up in the bed. He held out his hand, and I raised him up. He then said to the physicians: 'I feel myself going; I thank you for your attentions; but I pray you to take no more trouble about me. Let me go off quietly. I cannot last long.' They found that all which had been done was without effect. He lay down again, and all retired except Dr. Craik. He continued in the same situation, uneasy and restless, but without complaining, frequently asking what hour it was. When I helped him to move at this time, he did not speak, but looked at me with strong expressions of gratitude.

"About eight o'clock the physicians came again into the room, and applied blisters and cataplasms of wheat bran to his legs and feet, after which they went out, except Dr. Craik, without a ray of hope. I went out about this time, and wrote a line to Mr. Law and Mr. Peter, requesting them to come with their wives (Mrs. Washington's granddaughters) as soon as possible to Mount Vernon.

"About ten o'clock he made several attempts to speak to me before he could effect it. At length he said, 'I am just going. Have me decently buried; and do not let my body be put into the vault in less than three days after I am dead.' I bowed assent, for I could not speak. He then looked at me again and said, 'Do you understand me?' I replied, 'Yes.' ''Tis well,' said he.

"About ten minutes before he expired (which was between ten and eleven o'clock), his breathing became easier. He lay quietly; he withdrew his hand from mine, and felt his own pulse. I saw his countenance change. I spoke to Dr. Craik, who sat by the fire. He came to the bedside. The General's hand fell from his wrist. I took it in mine and pressed it to my bosom. Dr. Craik put his hands over his eyes, and he expired without a struggle or a sigh.

"While we were fixed in silent grief, Mrs. Washington, who was sitting at the foot of the bed, asked with a firm and collected voice, 'Is he gone?' I could not speak, but held up my hand, as a signal, that he was no more. ''Tis well,' said she, in the same voice, 'All is now over; I shall soon follow him; I have no more trials to pass through.' "

Such was the passing of Washington. On the afternoon of Wednesday, December 18, 1799, all that was mortal of this Cincinnatus of the West was laid to rest in the old tomb at Mount Vernon. The faithful Mr. Lear thus describes the funeral:

"Wednesday, December 18th. About eleven o'clock numbers of people began to assemble to attend the funeral, which was intended to have been at twelve o'clock; but, as a great part of the troops expected could not get down in time, it did not take place till three.

"Eleven pieces of artillery were brought from Alexandria; and a schooner belonging to Mr. R. Hamilton, came down and lay off Mount Vernon to fire minute guns.

"About three o'clock the procession began to move. The arrangements of the procession were made by Colonels Little, Simms, Deneale, and Dr. Dick. The pallbearers were Colonels Little, Payne, Gilpin, Ramsey, and Marsteller. Colonel Blackburn preceded the corpse. Colonel Deneale marched with the military. The procession moved out through the gate at the left wing of the house, and proceeded around in front of the lawn, and down to the vault on the right wing of the house. The procession was as follows:

The Troops, horse and foot.
The Clergy, namely, the Reverend Messrs. Davis, Muir, Maffitt, and Addison.
The General's horse, with his saddle, holsters, and pistols, led by two grooms, Cyrus and Wilson, in black.
The body, borne by the Freemasons and Officers.
Principal Mourners, namely,
Mrs. Stuart and Mrs. Law,
Misses Nancy and Sally Stuart,
Miss Fairfax and Miss Dennison,
Mr. Law and Mr. Peter,
Mr. Lear and Dr. Craik,
Lord Fairfax and Ferdinando Fairfax,
Lodge No. 22,
Corporation of Alexandria.
All other persons; preceded by Mr. Anderson and the Overseers.

"When the body arrived at the vault, the Rev. Mr. Davis read the service, and pronounced a short address.

"The Masons performed their ceremonies, and the body was deposited in the vault.

"After the ceremony, the company returned to the house, where they took some refreshment, and retired in good order."

After the death of General Washington, the family in Mount Vernon consisted of Mrs. Washington, Major Lawrence Lewis, nephew of Washington, and his wife, Nellie Lewis (nee Custis), their infant daughter, born shortly before the General's death, Tobias Lear and Albert Rawlins, the General's secretaries, and young George Washington Parke Custis. Mrs. Washington was deeply affected by her husband's death. She died, after an illness of several weeks duration, on May 22nd, 1802, and was laid to rest in the tomb at Mount Vernon. Lawrence and Nellie later removed to their beautiful mansion "Woodlawn"; and George Washington Parke Custis upon his marriage in 1804, took up his residence with his fair Virginia bride at Arlington, since famous as the home of his son-in-law, General Robert E. Lee, and the location of the Arlington National Cemetery.

Mount Vernon's Hallowed Tomb

Washington's will contained the following provision:

"The family vault at Mount Vernon requiring repairs, and being improperly situated besides, I desire that a new one, of brick and upon a larger scale, may be built at the foot of what is commonly called the vineyard enclosure,—on the ground which is marked out—, in which my remains, with those of my deceased relatives (now in the Old Vault) and such others of my family

79

as may choose to be entombed there, may be deposited."

The old tomb was "improperly situated" for the reason that, it was on a steep hillside at a place liable to slides. Besides, the tomb was damp, and its walls became parted by the roots of the trees which grew above it. The General's body lay in this tomb for almost thirty-one years, and during this time, the wooden covering of his leaden casket had to be replaced two times, owing to the dampness of the place.

About the year 1830, a vandal broke into the tomb in an unsuccessful attempt to steal the body of Washington, and this event stirred the surviving executors to action in carrying out the long delayed direction in his will. In 1831, the new tomb was constructed, and Washington's body, that of his wife, and those of all other deceased members of the Washington family in the old vault, were removed to this new resting place.

It was at the Old Tomb that Lafayette paid homage to the ashes of Washington, October 17th, 1824. On this occasion he was accompanied by his son George Washington Lafayette, Major Lawrence Lewis and George Washington Parke Custis. Mr. Custis presented him with a gold ring appropriately engraved and a lock of Washington's hair. His presentation speech was, in part, as follows:

"Last of the Generals of the Army of Independence, at this awful and impressive moment when forgetting the splendor of a triumph greater than the Roman Consul ever had, you bend with reverence over the remains of Washington, the child of Mount Vernon presents you with this token containing the hair of him, who while living you loved, and to whose honored grave you now pay this manly and affectionate tribute of a patriot and soldier's tear." Pressing the ring to his bosom the great Frenchman replied: "The feelings which at this awful moment oppress my heart do not leave the power of utterance; I can only thank you, my dear Custis, for your priceless gift, and pay silent homage to the tomb of the greatest and best of men—my paternal friend." Then he embraced Mr. Custis and the other gentlemen, and with tears streaming down his face, kissed the door of the vault, entered it and pressed his lips to the leaden casket of his old Commander. "Nothing," says Mr. Custis, "occurred to disturb the reverential solemnity of this leave-taking at the tomb. Not a soul intruded. The old oaks which grew round the sepulchre, touched with the mellow lustre of autumn, appeared as rich and ripe as the autumnal honors of Lafayette. Not a murmur was heard save the strains of solemn music and the deep measured sound of artillery, which woke the echoes around the hallowed heights of Mount Vernon."

In 1837, a vestibule was added to the front of the new tomb, and in it were placed, in sarcophagi hewn from Pennsylvania marble, and presented to the Washington family by Mr. John Struthers, of Philadelphia, the bodies of General and Mrs. Washington. It was on October 7, 1837, that Washington's coffin was placed in its marble sarcophagus, since which time it has never been disturbed.

The Historian, Benson J. Lossing, describes this event as follows:

"On entering the vault they found everything in confusion. Decayed fragments of coffins were scattered about, and bones of various parts of the human body were seen promiscuously thrown together. The decayed wood was dripping with moisture. The slimy snail glistened in the light of the door-opening. The brown centipede was disturbed by the admission of fresh air, and the mouldy case of the dead gave a pungent and unwholesome

OLD TOMB AT MOUNT VERNON RESTORED IN 1887

The original was built by George Washington shortly after the death of his half-brother Lawrence in 1752. In it Washington's body rested until 1831.

odor. The coffins of Washington and his lady were in the deepest recess of the vault. They were of lead, inclosed in wooden cases. When the sarcophagus arrived, the coffin of the chief was brought forth. The vault was first entered by Mr. Strickland, accompanied by Major Lewis (the last survivor of the first executors of the will of Washington) and his son. When the decayed wooden case was removed, the leaden lid was perceived to be sunken and fractured. In the bottom of the wooden case was found a silver coffin-plate, in the form of a shield, which was placed upon the leaden coffin when Washington was first entombed. 'At the request of Major Lewis,' says Mr. S., 'the fractured part of the lid was turned over on the lower part, exposing to view a head and breast of large dimensions, which appeared, by the dim light of the

NEW TOMB AT MOUNT VERNON, BUILT IN 1831

The vestibule in front was added in 1837, and in it, in marble Sarcophagi, rest the bodies of General and Martha Washington. The remains of many of the Washington and Custis families are in the back part of the tomb, which is separated from the vestibule by an iron door.

candles, to have suffered but little from the effects of time. The eye-sockets were large and deep, and the breadth across the temples, together with the forehead, appeared of unusual size. There was no appearance of grave-clothes; the chest was broad, the color was dark, and had the appearance of dried flesh and skin adhering closely to the bones. We saw no hair, nor was there any offensive odor from the body; but we observed, when the coffin had been removed to the outside of the vault, the dripping down of a yellow liquid, which stained the marble of the sarcophagus. A hand was laid upon the

THE FAMOUS HOUDON STATUE OF WASHINGTON
Life-sized statue of Washington which adorns the State Capitol at Richmond, Virginia. The sculptor was Jean A. Houdon, who was sent to America from Paris, by Benjamin Franklin.

head and instantly removed; the leaden lid was restored to its place; the body, raised by six men, was carried and laid in a marble coffin, and the ponderous cover being put on and set in cement, it was sealed from our sight on Saturday, the 7th day of October, 1837. . . . . . the relatives who were present, consisting of Major Lewis, Lorenzo Lewis, John Augustine Washington, George Washington, the Rev. Mr. Johnson and lady, and Mrs. Jane Washington, then retired to the mansion."

The proposal to move Washington's body to Washington City and place it under the dome of the Capitol was agitated shortly after his death. President John Adams made such request of Mrs. Washington, and she consented, but the project was shortly abandoned. Once more, in 1832, when the nation celebrated the centennial of his birth, Congress renewed the request made over thirty years before by President Adams; and a platform was prepared in the crypt under the dome of the Capitol upon which the sarcophagus of Washington was to rest; but his relatives refused to grant permission for the removal of the remains on the ground that the General had made it plain in his will that he desired his body to repose in the quiet of his beloved Mount Vernon.

Vessels passing up and down the Potomac toll the bell when they come opposite the tomb of Washington. This custom is said to have originated on August 24, 1814, when the British fleet sailed up the river. Instead of attacking Mount Vernon, Captain Gordon of the Royal Navy had the seven ships of his fleet to fire salutes as they came abreast, although at the time, England and the United States were at war. Also when war ships of the United States Navy come abreast the tomb, the crews stand at attention as a mark of respect to the memory of the honored dead.

Here, then, in his unpretentious tomb, on his own farm, on the banks of his long-loved Potomac, "after life's fitful fever, he sleeps well." He has monuments of marble and bronze, medals of silver and gold; but his best monument is the best love of the best American hearts, and the truest impression of his image is in the improved condition of mankind, which came about as the fruits of the immortal principles which he championed. The centuries shall place tributes on his bier and at his tomb. He shall abide as a power for all time. His image shall cast itself on the current of the ages as the mountain mirrors its form in the river that winds at its foot—the mighty fixing itself immutably upon the changing.

THE END.

INDEX

———

87

INDEX

Some Comments of the Press and Testimonial Letters after the appearance of the first Edition of this volume.

WELL WRITTEN AND HISTORICALLY CORRECT

"Mount Vernon and The Washington Family" is a concise handbook on the ancestry, youth and family of George Washington and the history of his home. It is written to fill the gap that has hitherto existed in literature on Washington by reason of there being no short work on the history of his family, his home at Mount Vernon and his life there.

The booklet is well written, printed in an easy readable type, and further enhanced by many full page half tone illustrations. It also contains a complete index.

The author has been a student of Washington for years and has spent much time in painstaking search of records so that this work is historically correct. It is primarily intended for the busy reader who does not have time to peruse voluminous works on this most interesting subject.—*From Pittsburgh Legal Journal of July 5, 1924.*

PRAISED BY HISTORICAL EXPERTS

This work on the Washingtons and Mount Vernon has been praised by historical experts.—*The Literary Digest.*

A BOOK THAT MEETS A LACK

The galaxy of men who were the leaders in the convention which adopted the Declaration of Independence, and in the Constitutional Convention is not surpassed in human history; and in practical wisdom and unselfish devotion to the cause of the colonies George Washington surpassed them all. No doubt it was because of these two qualities that Gladstone said Washington "is the purest figure in history"; and it is this combination that causes America to honor and reverence Washington and to hold Mount Vernon as her one great shrine.

The author of this little booklet, feeling this, has written a concise history of the Washington family from 1183, when William de Hertburn received a grant of the manor of Wessyngton, which took on its final form as Washington. He has also given a brief history of Mount Vernon.

This booklet meets a lack. It is written in simple, concise language, and beautifully printed and illustrated.—*Boston Transcript of August 23, 1924.*

AN EXCELLENT PIECE OF WORK

HENRY W. ELSON, the noted historian, author of Elson's United States History, Side Lights on American History, and Modern Times and The Living Past, writes as follows:

"It is an excellent piece of work. Your terse and direct way of saying what you want to say attracts the reader and clearly conveys the meaning intended. It is the best short account of the Washingtons and Mount Vernon that I have seen. It deserves a large sale."

AN INTERESTING BOOK

EX-PRESIDENT WILLIAM HOWARD TAFT, Chief Justice of the Supreme Court of the United States, writes:

"I have read it with interest."

AN INSTRUCTIVE BOOK

EARL SPENCER whose ancestral seat is Althrop Manor in Northamptonshire, England, only a few miles from Sulgrave Manor, the ancient home of the Washingtons, writes from Spencer House, under date of November 16, 1924:

"I am greatly interested in Mount Vernon and the Washington Family and have been greatly instructed by reading it, having learned a lot about the family."

AN ACCURATE AND ELOQUENT BOOK

HON. W. H. S. THOMSON, Judge of the United States District Court for the Western District of Pennsylvania, writes:

"I have read your little volume with great interest. Dealing with facts gathered from a wide field of research, you were evidently impressed with the thought that historical accuracy was the one thing needful. You have put in condensed form in logical arrangement, and with eloquent simplicity of expression, much that all Americans should know touching the life of this great historical figure. At once interesting and instructive, the volume deserves a very wide circulation."

OF INTEREST TO EVERY AMERICAN

HON. THEODORE E. BURTON, Congressman and former United States Senator from Ohio, writes:

"Even though small, it contains much of interest to every American. I thoroughly enjoyed it."

A BOOK EVERY AMERICAN SHOULD READ

HON. ARTHUR CAPPER, Editor of Capper's Weekly, and United States Senator from Kansas, writes:

"I have been very much interested in reading your booklet on the Washington family, and congratulate you upon the presentation of this reliable bit of true American history. Some of the facts related by you are new to me, and I enjoyed them greatly. This is a volume which it would be well for all Americans to read, and I hope it has an exceptionally wide circulation."

A BOOK THAT SHOULD BE IN EVERY SCHOOL

F. W. HODGE, of the Smithsonian Institution and the Museum of the American Indian, writes as follows:

"I have derived great pleasure from reading 'Mount Vernon and the Washington Family'. This story is so succinctly and well told that I wish it could be placed in every school library in the land and listed as required reading by members of all boys' and girls' organizations. It should make better citizens."

___

AN ACCURATE AND SCHOLARLY WORK

REV. RICHARD B. WASHINGTON, Hot Springs, Virginia, a collateral descendant of George Washington, writes as under date of May 10, 1929:

"I am very much pleased, indeed, to know that you are about to publish the fifth edition of your very fine book, 'Mount Vernon and the Washington Family'. I consider it a most accurate and scholarly work.

___

OTHER HISTORICAL WORKS BY C. HALE SIPE

"The Indian Chiefs of Pennsylvania"

A Story of the Part Played by the American Indian in the History of Pennsylvania, Based Primarily on the Pennsylvania Archives and Colonial Records and Built Around the Outstanding Chiefs. Introduction by Dr. George P. Donehoo, former State Librarian of Pennsylvania; Collaborator of the Handbook of American Indians, Bureau of American Ethnology, Smithsonian Institution.

"The Indian Chiefs of Pennsylvania" contains 569 pages, chronological table of 300 events and index. Published in April, 1927, it has attained a larger circulation than any other specialized history relating to Pennsylvania. A valuable book for the lover of informative literature, it appeals especially to educators and historians. It is in 42 colleges and universities and several hundred high schools in Pennsylvania, as well as in more than one hundred colleges and universities outside of Pennsylvania, including several universities in Europe.

Price $5.00, post paid. Order from C. HALE SIPE, P. O. Box 536, Butler, Pa.

___

"The Indian Wars of Pennsylvania"

An Account of the Indian Events, in Pennsylvania, of The French and Indian War, Pontiac's War, Lord Dunmore's War, The Revolutionary War and the Indian Uprisings from 1789 to 1795.

This beautifully illustrated history of 750 pages, with chronological table of 400 events and index, is based primarily on the Pennsylvania Archives and Colonial Records. It is an accurate and authoritative history.

This is the only history of the Great Indian Wars and Uprisings in Pennsylvania ever published. Contains accurate accounts of the hundreds of battles and tragedies on the Pennsylvania frontier. Every college, university and public library in the United States should have this authoritative history.

Introduction by Dr. George P. Donehoo, former State Librarian of Pennsylvania.

Published in 1929. More than 1,000 orders for this history in advance of publication, many of them from the leading colleges and universities in America.

Price $5.00, post paid. Order from C. HALE SIPE, P. O. Box 536 Butler, Pa.